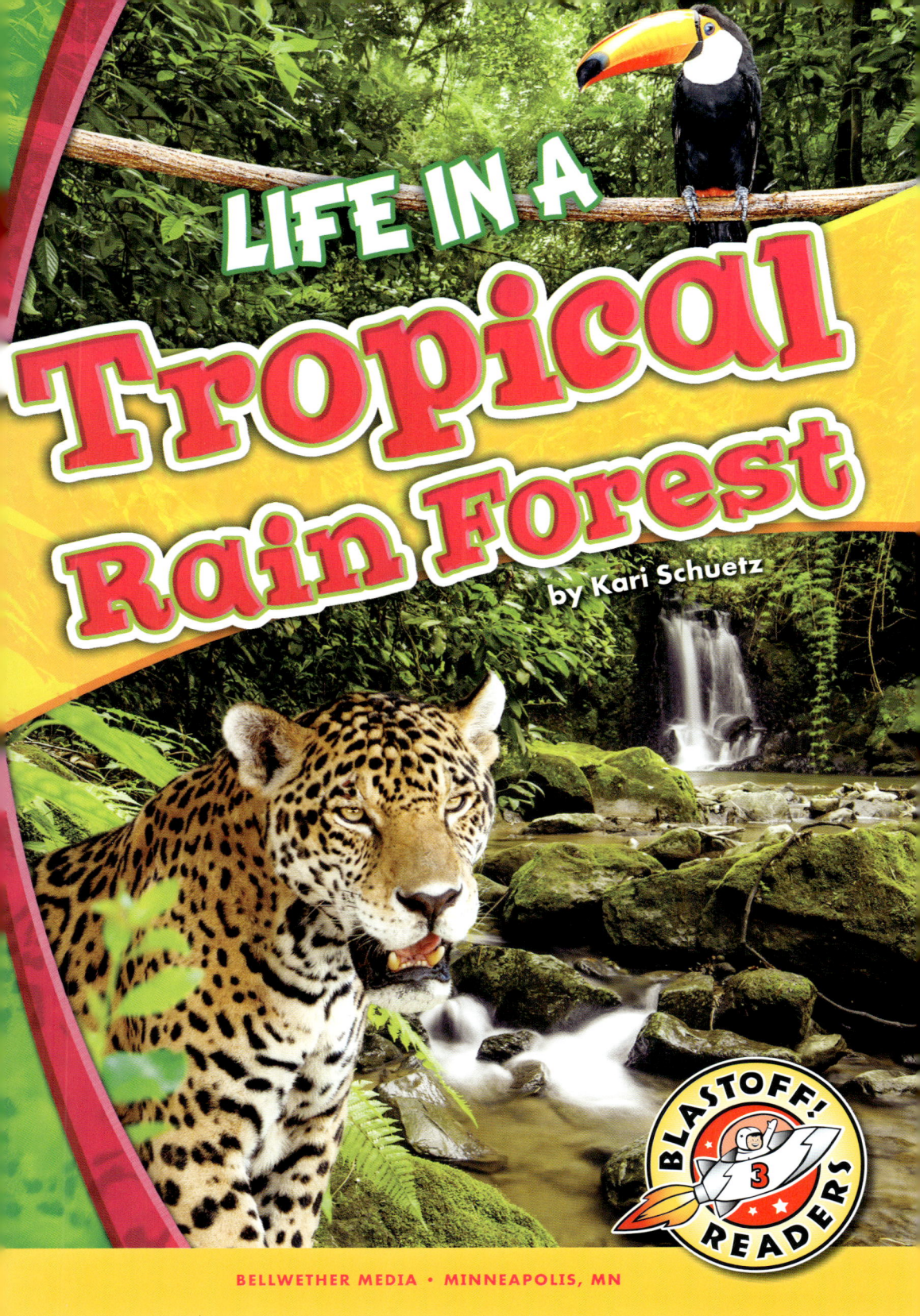

Note to Librarians, Teachers, and Parents:

**Blastoff! Readers** are carefully developed by literacy experts and combine standards-based content with developmentally appropriate text.

**Level 1** provides the most support through repetition of high-frequency words, light text, predictable sentence patterns, and strong visual support.

**Level 2** offers early readers a bit more challenge through varied simple sentences, increased text load, and less repetition of high-frequency words.

**Level 3** advances early-fluent readers toward fluency through increased text and concept load, less reliance on visuals, longer sentences, and more literary language.

**Level 4** builds reading stamina by providing more text per page, increased use of punctuation, greater variation in sentence patterns, and increasingly challenging vocabulary.

**Level 5** encourages children to move from "learning to read" to "reading to learn" by providing even more text, varied writing styles, and less familiar topics.

Whichever book is right for your reader, Blastoff! Readers are the perfect books to build confidence and encourage a love of reading that will last a lifetime!

This edition first published in 2016 by Bellwether Media, Inc.

No part of this publication may be reproduced in whole or in part without written permission of the publisher. For information regarding permission, write to Bellwether Media, Inc., Attention: Permissions Department, 5357 Penn Avenue South, Minneapolis, MN 55419.

Library of Congress Cataloging-in-Publication Data

Schuetz, Kari, author.
 Life in a Tropical Rain Forest / by Kari Schuetz.
    pages cm. – (Blastoff! Readers. Biomes Alive!)
  Summary: "Simple text and full-color photography introduce beginning readers to life in a tropical rain forest. Developed by literacy experts for students in kindergarten through third grade"– Provided by publisher.
  Audience: Ages 5-8.
  Audience: K to grade 3.
  Includes bibliographical references and index.
  ISBN 978-1-62617-320-0 (hardcover : alk. paper)
 1. Rain forest ecology–Juvenile literature. 2. Rain forest animals–Juvenile literature. 3. Amazon River Region–Juvenile literature.  I. Title.
 QH541.5.R27S38 2016
 577.34–dc23
                                             2015034276

Text copyright © 2016 by Bellwether Media, Inc. BLASTOFF! READERS and associated logos are trademarks and/or registered trademarks of Bellwether Media, Inc. SCHOLASTIC, CHILDREN'S PRESS, and associated logos are trademarks and/or registered trademarks of Scholastic Inc.

Printed in the United States of America, North Mankato, MN.

# Table of Contents

| | |
|---|---|
| The Tropical Rain Forest Biome | 4 |
| The Climate | 8 |
| The Plants | 12 |
| The Animals | 16 |
| The Amazon Rain Forest | 20 |
| Glossary | 22 |
| To Learn More | 23 |
| Index | 24 |

# The Tropical Rain Forest Biome

Bali rain forest

The tropical rain forest is one of Earth's wet **biomes**! It is green and full of life.

More than 15 million kinds of plants and animals may live in its rivers, mountains, and valleys!

red-eyed tree frog

Tropical rain forests lie by the **equator**. Half of them belong to **Latin America**. This includes the Amazon rain forest, the world's largest.

Amazon rain forest

More rain forests once existed on Earth. But loggers have cut many down for wood and farmland.

# The Climate

Reunion Island rain forest

All tropical rain forests have a warm **climate**. Temperatures stay around 80 degrees Fahrenheit (27 degrees Celsius) throughout the year.

Every day has 12 hours of daylight. But trees shade the ground from sunlight.

Braulio Carrillo National Park, Costa Rica

Everything stays wet in the rain forest. The air is **humid** and **dew** collects on plants.

passionflower

Borneo rain forest

**Precipitation** falls on most days. More than 100 inches (254 centimeters) of rain is possible in a year!

# The Plants

emergent

canopy

The top of a rain forest is called the **canopy**. Trees stretch 100 feet (30 meters) or more into the sky. **Emergents** reach even higher.

The **understory** and forest floor are the middle and bottom layers. Shorter trees and plants have **adapted** to survive with less light and a lot of water.

Some plants like vines climb trees to find sunlight. Ferns and orchids grow on tree trunks and branches to get sun.

orchid

vine

bromeliad

air plant

Many plants hold rainwater with their waxy leaves. Plants with aboveground **roots** collect wetness from the air.

# The Animals

jaguar

walking leaf insect

In rain forests, many animals use **camouflage** to blend in with trees and flowers. Both hunters and the hunted want to stay hidden.

**Poisonous** animals are often bright red or yellow. Their colors warn others to stay away.

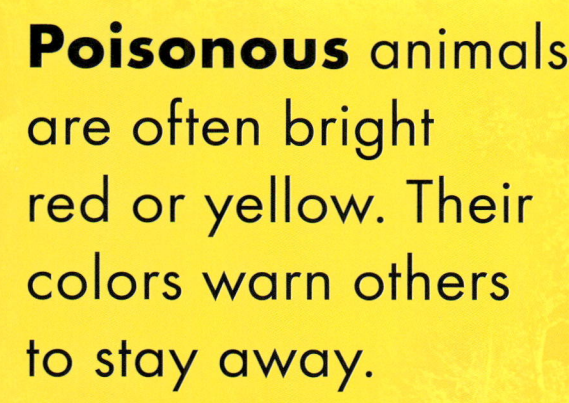

golden poison frog

postman butterfly

toucan

two-toed sloth

Most rain forest animals live in the canopy. Its full trees provide food and shelter.

Tree-dwellers have strong legs to climb, jump, or hang from branches. Their loud voices call to one another!

red howler monkeys

# The Amazon Rain Forest

**Location:** South America; Bolivia, Brazil, Colombia, Ecuador, Guyana, Peru, Suriname, Venezuela, and French Guiana

**Size:** 2.3 million square miles (6 million square kilometers); largest tropical rain forest in the world

**Temperature:** around 80 °F (27 °C)

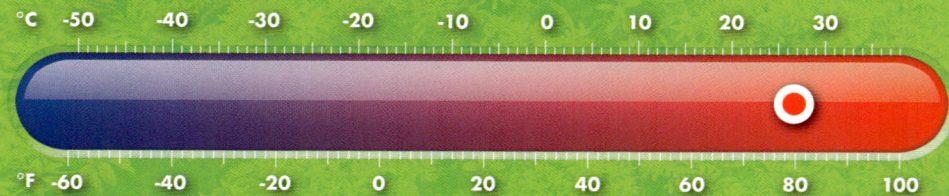

**Precipitation:** 60 to 175 inches (152 to 445 centimeters) per year

# AMAZON RAIN FOREST FOOD WEB

**Other important plants:** kapok trees, rubber trees, acacia trees, palms, vines, ferns, orchids, mosses

**Other important animals:** spider monkeys, macaws, toucans, capybaras, caimans, giant river otters, poison dart frogs

# Glossary

**adapted**—changed to survive in new conditions

**biomes**—nature communities defined by their climate, land features, and living things

**camouflage**—a way of using color to blend in with surroundings

**canopy**—the top of a rain forest; the tallest trees in a rain forest form the canopy.

**climate**—the specific weather conditions for an area

**dew**—water droplets that appear on plants when the air is full of wetness

**emergents**—trees that rise above the surrounding canopy

**equator**—the imaginary line that divides Earth into northern and southern halves

**humid**—having a lot of wetness in the air

**Latin America**—a region made up of North and South American countries that lie south of the United States

**poisonous**—having a liquid that can harm or kill

**precipitation**—water that falls to the earth from the sky

**roots**—the parts of a plant that hold it in place and take in water

**understory**—the layer of a forest below the canopy and above the forest floor

# To Learn More

**AT THE LIBRARY**
Amstutz, Lisa J. *Rain Forest Animal Adaptations*. Mankato, Minn.: Capstone Press, 2012.

Amstutz, Lisa J. *What Eats What in a Rain Forest Food Chain*. North Mankato, Minn.: Picture Window Books, 2013.

Rice, William. *Amazon Rainforest*. New York, N.Y.: TIME for Kids, 2012.

**ON THE WEB**
Learning more about tropical rain forests is as easy as 1, 2, 3.

1. Go to www.factsurfer.com.

2. Enter "tropical rain forests" into the search box.

3. Click the "Surf" button and you will see a list of related web sites.

With factsurfer.com, finding more information is just a click away.

# Index

Amazon rain forest, 6
animal adaptations, 16, 17, 19
animals, 5, 16, 17, 18, 19
branches, 14, 19
canopy, 12, 13, 18
climate, 4, 8, 10, 11, 15
dew, 10
emergents, 12
equator, 6, 7
farmland, 7
forest floor, 13
Latin America, 6
layers, 12, 13
leaves, 15
location, 6, 7
loggers, 7
mountains, 5
plant adaptations, 13, 14, 15
plants, 5, 9, 10, 12, 13, 14, 15, 16, 18, 19
precipitation, 11, 15
rivers, 5
roots, 15
sunlight, 9, 13, 14
temperatures, 8
trunks, 14
understory, 13
valleys, 5
water, 13, 15
wood, 7

The images in this book are reproduced through the courtesy of: Patryk Kosmider, front cover (jaguar); MarcusVDT, front cover (toucan); William Berry, front cover (background); Michele Falzone/ JAI/ Corbis, p. 4; Minden Pictures/ SuperStock, pp. 5, 19; thobo, p. 6; Loop Images/ SuperStock, p. 8; Peter Schnickert/ Age Fotostock/ SuperStock, p. 9; SuperStock/ Glow Images, p. 10; Thomas Marent/ ardea.com/ Pant/ Pantheon/ SuperStock/ Minden Pictures/ Corbis, pp. 11, 16 (bottom), 17 (left); Salparadis, p. 12; Bellwether Media, p. 13; Mps197, p. 14 (left); PhilipYb Studio, p. 14 (right); Kajornyot, p. 15 (right); FLPA/ SuperStock, p. 15 (left); ANDRE DIB, p. 16; Marythepooh, p. 17 (right); Luciano Queiroz, p. 18 (top); TanArt, p. 18 (bottom); Ammit Jack, p. 20; Pal Teravagimov, p. 21 (jaguar); Patrick K. Campbell, p. 21 (green anaconda); Tonny Wu, p. 21 (two-toed sloth); Volodymyr Sergeiev, p. 21 (agouti); goldenjack, p. 21 (bromeliad); Brasil2, p. 21 (brazil nut tree).